Old St Bees

by
Donald A. Brownrigg

This book is dedicated to the people of St Bees, past, present and future.

The largest vessel to be wrecked at St Bees, the SS *Izaro*, ran aground in thick fog at the foot of Tomlin on 20 May 1907 carrying a cargo of iron ore (see also pages 36 and 37).

West Doorway, St. Bees Church
A. D. 1158.

First published in the United Kingdom, 2003,
by Stenlake Publishing
Telephone / Fax: 01290 551122

ISBN 1 84033 254 9

ACKNOWLEDGEMENTS

Thanks to Doug Sim for permission to use material from his book *100 Years of St Bees*, as well as from articles he has written. I would also like to thank Dr Ian McAndrew and Dr John Todd for contributing information relating to the St Bees Man. In several places I have reproduced quotes about village life in the early twentieth century collected and published under the guidance of John Todd as part of his local history class in 1984 – my thanks are extended to those who contributed their recollections to this project. Thanks also to Malcolm Reid for his assistance, and to the people who provided the illustrations on the following pages: Mrs Moorhouse: 15 (upper), 18 (lower), 37, 39, 44; St Bees School: back cover; RNLI: 29; Val Turpin: 41; Eleanor Haile: 40; Mrs Lynne Murphy: 28 (upper); Irene Patterson: 19; Dr Ian McAndrew: 4, 5. Special thanks are due to Doug Sim and Chris Robson for their help in checking over the manuscript.

The magnificent west door of St Bees Priory Church dates from *c*.1160, and is richly carved with successive arcades of chevrons featuring several beakheads of birds and beasts. The arcades rise from intricately carved capitals, beneath which there would have originally been sandstone pillars, although only one of these survives. Apart form some obvious modern restoration work to the right, the doorway has changed little in 800 years. Inside the church, opposite the door, is an alcove with a Norman lintel stone showing a fight between St Michael and a dragon, which towers over St Michael threateningly. The stone dates from *c*.1120 and may originally have been installed over the entrance to an earlier church or chapel. In the alcove is a cross which stood at the breast of the hill on the main road to Whitehaven. It is variously thought to be a 'sanctuary' cross, marking the boundary of the parish, or a resting cross on a coffin road. The coffin roads date from medieval times when many West Cumbrian parishes did not have the licence to bury, and bodies were brought to St Bees for burial from as far away as Ennerdale and Eskdale. These crosses served as symbolic resting-places.

INTRODUCTION

There is something about the village of St Bees that gives it a quite different character from that of any other seaside resort of similar size. Its origins lie in the legend of an Irish princess – Bega – who is said to have fled her native land around AD 850 having been promised in marriage by her father to the son of a king of Norway. Having crossed the Irish Sea, she made landfall at the place that later took the name of St Bees, where she led a life of exemplary piety until forced to flee inland by Viking raiders.

Soon after 1120 a Benedictine Priory was founded and dedicated to St Bega, whose principal relic was a bracelet or ring which was kept at St Bees. The Priory was a dependency of St Mary's Abbey at York until its dissolution on 16 October 1539. At this time it was referred to as the 'cell of St Bees', a description which would have been in keeping with the saint's status as an anchoress. These religious recluses (the male equivalent was an anchorite), who usually came from wealthy families, undertook a life of isolation within a small stone room or cell, which was often attached to a church or larger religious establishment. The cell had a small window, but no door (its occupant was frequently bricked in), and the window was generally covered by a curtain to prevent the outside world from distracting the anchoress or anchorite from their life of religious observance.

Saintly relics were enormously valuable to institutions such as priories, attracting pilgrims to them and also securing donations. Only one relic belonging to Bega, a bracelet, is known to have been held at the Priory of St Bees. It is mentioned in the early thirteenth century when Robert de Vipont and his wife Idonea pledged 'to God and the church of St Mary the Virgin in which the bracelet was kept' a rent of ten shillings a year. Oaths were taken on the bracelet, an ancient pagan practice. Of the nine miracles recorded in the *Life of St Bega*, three mention the power of her bracelet, which she is believed to have brought over from Ireland. It may have been a flat ribbon type, which was associated with Ireland and Wales during the ninth and tenth centuries, and which was often stamped with a St Andrew's cross. Similar bracelets have also been found in Lancashire and Kirkcudbright.

The best-known miracle concerning St Bega tells of one Ranulf le Meschin, whose brother William had endowed the Priory with its lands. A dispute about their extent apparently arose later and a lawsuit developed, prompting concerns amongst the monks who occupied the Priory about a miscarriage of justice. On the day appointed for walking the Priory boundaries – and thus determining their extent – snow had fallen thickly on the ground around the Priory but left its own lands untouched, thereby seeming to define their extent divinely. John Todd points out that the tale may not be entirely fanciful, even if the coincidence of the snowfall with the occasion of the checking of the boundaries is unlikely. He comments: 'it is within the experience of West Cumbrians that a sudden snowstorm may sweep along the coast and miss St Bees Head and the land immediately behind it'. A second and less plausible snow miracle relates how Bega asked the lord of Egremont for some land, and he laughingly promised her as much as would be covered by snow the following day, Midsummer Day. Snow is then said to have duly fallen, covering only that area of land within about three miles of where the Priory was later to be situated.

Whatever the precise details of the early life of St Bega, it is likely that the secular settlement of St Bees originated as a number of scattered farms along the road south from the Priory. Following its dissolution by Henry VIII, the centre of gravity of St Bees moved southwards where there was more land suitable for building. The foundation of St Bees School in 1583 and the establishment of the theological college in 1816 are probably the two most important factors in the village's subsequent growth and consolidation. The nineteenth century saw the building of a number of terraces of houses – notably Hampton Place – to cater for the 30 to 50 theological students that would be in lodgings in the village at any one time. In 1849 the arrival of the Furness Railway brought tourism to St Bees, leading to the establishment of hotels such as the Royal at the railway station, the Albert, the Seacote and the Queens. Around this time St Bees also saw the advent of the commuter. By the late 1800s the village's Main Street had taken on its modern appearance. Today St Bees is an attractive and vibrant village, with an unusually distinguished history for a settlement of its size.

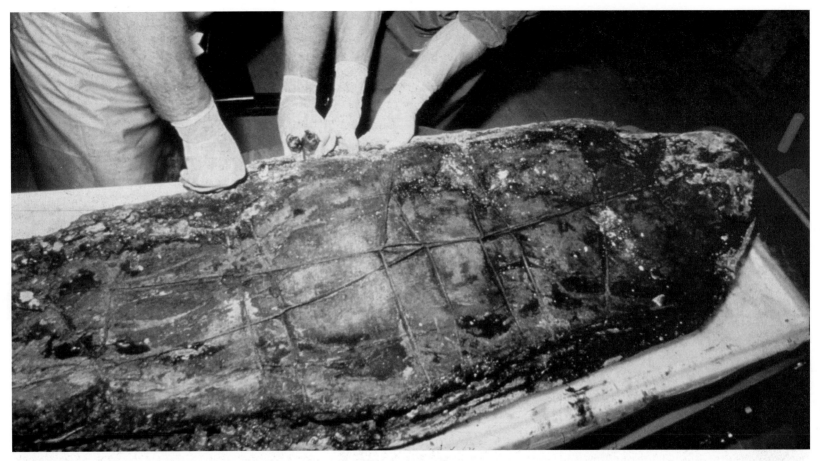

During 1981, the third year of a series of archaeological investigations at St Bees, a dig was carried out in what had formerly been an aisle within the chancel of the Priory Church that had been roofless and disused since *c*.1500. Soon after the excavation began the floor level of the chancel aisle was determined, and various pottery pieces from the fourteenth century were found, along with burials from before and after the aisle was built. All these burials, with one exception, were skeletons. In the middle of the aisle, in front of where the altar had once stood, a vault was found and amongst the clay in this was a lead coffin or wrapper. It was thought unlikely that this would contain anything more than a skeleton, especially as the lead was damaged at the foot, but when it was removed – to everyone's amazement – what appeared to be a solid body, neatly parcelled in twine and linen, was revealed. Fortunately both the local GP and undertaker were in attendance at the time and were able to quickly arrange for the body to be transferred to cold storage at the local hospital.

A rapid and successful application for funds from the Department of the Environment paid for the services of Dr Eddie Tapp, a paleopathologist from Preston Royal Infirmary, to examine the body. The post-mortem examination, which took place over two days, revealed that it had been wrapped in linen coated with a resinous substance (probably beeswax) and this, plus other factors, had resulted in the extensive formation of adipocere, a fatty or soapy substance which is formed in corpses under certain conditions of cold and dampness (though rarely to this degree). This had preserved the body's organs and tissues in such detail that it was possible not only to determine the man's cause of death, but also his state of general health prior to the injuries that had killed him. The skin, where not stained by the wrapping cloth, was still pinkish. When cut, the tissues were very similar to those of someone recently deceased and liquid blood was found in the chest cavity.

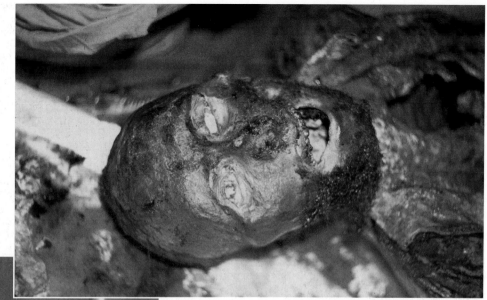

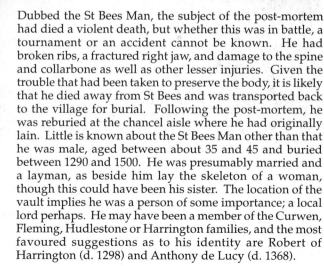

Dubbed the St Bees Man, the subject of the post-mortem had died a violent death, but whether this was in battle, a tournament or an accident cannot be known. He had broken ribs, a fractured right jaw, and damage to the spine and collarbone as well as other lesser injuries. Given the trouble that had been taken to preserve the body, it is likely that he died away from St Bees and was transported back to the village for burial. Following the post-mortem, he was reburied at the chancel aisle where he had originally lain. Little is known about the St Bees Man other than that he was male, aged between about 35 and 45 and buried between 1290 and 1500. He was presumably married and a layman, as beside him lay the skeleton of a woman, though this could have been his sister. The location of the vault implies he was a person of some importance; a local lord perhaps. He may have been a member of the Curwen, Fleming, Hudlestone or Harrington families, and the most favoured suggestions as to his identity are Robert of Harrington (d. 1298) and Anthony de Lucy (d. 1368).

The path called Pitman's Trod (foreground) led over to Loughrigg and was used by miners walking between St Bees and the iron ore mines in the Egremont area. This halftone view was published c.1894. The technique of converting continuous tone images (photographs), into halftones (comprised of dots of ink of varying sizes), allowed the mass reproduction of photographic images on printing presses. This one was produced from a photograph by Green Brothers of Grasmere, and was accompanied by the following caption, describing St Bees: 'This little town, four miles south of Whitehaven, is very picturesquely situated, and possesses several points of interest. Its noble Priory church formerly belonged to the Benedictines, and is built on the site of a former Culdee settlement which was destroyed in an invasion by the Danes. There is a Theological College here, established by Law in 1816, for educating ministers for the Church of England who cannot afford the University course.'

The view from Whitehaven Road c.1900, with a Furness Railway locomotive leaving the station and the new buildings of the rapidly expanding St Bees School in the foreground. In the distance is the old gasworks. During the Jacobite rising of 1745, Prince Charles Edward Stuart, the Young Pretender, marched into England at the head of a rising which intended to dethrone King George II. As it passed through Cumberland, his army split in two, reassembling again at Kendal, with one party passing near St Bees. Several boys ran away from the school to join the Scots despite the opposition of the headmaster, a partisan of King George.

MAIN STREET, ST BEES

This postcard of Main Street (printed by J. Whalley of St Bees) was posted in May 1924 to West Park, Leeds. The writer says that he has found rooms with 'all conveniences' in a house (Granger House) at the top of Little Lane leading to Blythe Place, adding that the cost is £1 per room per week and telling the recipient 'well recommended'. In 1816 a theological college was established at St Bees for the training of north country candidates who wished to take holy orders. The college was set up under the auspices of the Right Revd George Henry Law, Bishop of Chester, while a generous gift from the 1st Earl of Lonsdale made it possible to reconstruct the chancel of the Priory Church for use as a great hall, library and lecture room for the new college. This was the first college for the training of Church of England clergy outside the universities of Oxford and Cambridge, and by the time of its closure in 1895 over 2,500 clergy had been trained there. The foundation of the college brought extra income to the village in the form of lodgers who needed accommodation during the period of their training. The terrace on the right, Hampton Place, was built as a result of the demand for lodgings. Apart from the absence of ranks of parked cars, the Main Street of today looks little different from this 1920s view. Most of its houses date from the nineteenth century, although Nursery House is probably of seventeenth century origin. Along with Manor House and Stonehouse Farm it illustrates how older buildings were set back much further from the line of the street as it exists today. In 1850 the village had 21 farms, many of them situated along Main Street, but by 1950 this number had dropped to eight.

Edward and Mary Ann Wilson ran a greengrocer's and poultry dealer's shop from 1880 to 1910 at No. 4 Main Street, the building on the right with the round plaque above the front door (this originally had the shop sign attached to it). Chickens and rabbits, ready dressed, hung by the door. The barber's shop in the foreground at No. 7 was run by Edward Morgan from 1910 to 1920. His daughter Nita assisted him and later married John McNeal, whose father was a stonemason and lived at Fleswick House. After 1920 Herbert Reace took over the shop and charged 3d for a haircut and shave. Main Street's numbers start at the bottom of the street on the right as seen in this picture and increase to the top of the street, where they then continue down the other side, with the highest numbers allotted to the buildings on the left in this picture. The water fountain in the left foreground was given to St Bees by John Kenworthy when he closed the access route to the West Well, and the house it was attached to became known as Fountain House. The fountain was removed some time ago and is now in Malcolm Reid's garden at Meadow House.

In 1880 the tuck shop on Main Street (visible in the middle distance on the left, with the laburnum tree outside) was run by Mrs Nicholson. From 1900 to 1925 two sisters ran it, Isabella and Hannah Nash, and are remembered for the shortbread biscuits they made. Emma Reid, grandmother of Malcolm Reid, owned the business until 1940, then her daughter-in-law Dinah Haile took it over. James Haile put up the sign 'Tuck Shop' and altered the window, but the laburnum tree was cut down by another owner. Stonehouse Farm, centre right, was originally owned by the Earl of Lonsdale. Prior to the Second World War he was the major landowner in the village, but the crushing death duties payable by his family following his death led to the breaking up of his estates in the mid-1950s, at which point the St Bees lands were bought by the county council. In the 1960s it was a common sight to see Joe Smith driving his cattle to and from Stonehouse Farm for milking. Grindal House (left foreground) was originally built as the Station Hotel. It was bought by St Bees School in 1888, and every evening during term time at 10 p.m. the last post was sounded from its balcony to signal lights out for the school's boarders. This was answered with a bugle call from Foundation House on the north side of the valley.

This is one of Robert Broomfield's 'Sancta Bega' series of postcards dating from *c*.1900. In the middle distance on the left is Broomfield's chemist's shop, which was also the telephone exchange and telegraph office (the telephone mast is visible on the building above the shop). The original line of Main Street at its upper end was regraded in the mid-1800s to make it less steep for quarry traffic. Mrs Margaret Charters, a widow, kept a sweet shop at 44 Main Street (until recently the doctor's surgery) in the front room of her house, situated behind the railings on the left of the picture, and served children from the window. The small ledge under the window is worn down through them standing on it for a better view of the wares. At Christmas she stocked small toys too. This 'fancy' repository existed from 1910 to 1920. The house on the extreme left belonged to Mr Ireland, manager of the St Bees Gas Co.

This postcard of the Main Street was sent in July 1906 and shows Broomfield's chemist's on the left. John Reay was the first and best-known dispensing chemist in St Bees and was in business from 1850 to 1890. He was also photographer and bookseller to the theological college, and sold not only toiletries, medicines, stationery and lithographic prints, but also wines, aerated waters, magazines, tobacco, bibles, novels, pianos and perfumes. His successor from c.1890 to 1914 was Robert Broomfield, who would either prescribe medicines himself or summon a doctor by phone: Dr Harry Braithwaite would come from Egremont in his car, while Dr Mitchell cycled from Beech House, also in Egremont. Afterwards the shop became a chemist's and paper shop run by Albert Ashby, and was run from 1920 to 1930 by William Whalley. In later years John Fee, father of garage proprietor Gill Fee, ran the shop. The village's telephone exchange was installed on the premises in the early 1900s. This was of course a manual exchange and Howard Smith recalls that in the early days there were very few lines, with the highest phone number being 26. Phone calls after 6 p.m. were discouraged. Fred Chinner remembers the Stephen's Ink thermometer that was on the wall outside Broomfield's. This is still in the possession of the present owners of the shop, Neil and Gay Bettinson.

Produced by Robert Broomfield, the then chemist in St Bees, this photograph dates from the late 1890s and shows the front door and occupants of 4 Vale View. On the 1891 census sheet for Vale View the head of the house is listed as John Dalziel Kenworthy, then aged 32 and seen here with his three children and two unidentified women. Born in Whitehaven in 1858, he was a portrait and rustic painter in oil and watercolour. He became a professional artist, showing his work at the Royal Academy as well as locally, and was elected an Associate of the Royal Cambrian Academy in 1914. Of his three children, the oldest was Stanley, who died in action at Montauban in France in 1916. Neither his second son Gordon nor his daughter Laura married, and he has no direct descendants. Gordon entered the church and ultimately became rector of Wokingham in Berkshire. Around 1900 his father left Vale View and purchased Seacroft House. He died in 1954. Stanley Kenworthy (the inset portrait is by his father), was a captain in the 17th Battalion of the Manchester Regiment and died at the Somme on 1 July 1916 at the age of 32. He is buried in Dantzig Alley British cemetery in Mametz, Somme (the cemetery is named after a German trench). Mametz was taken by the 7th Division on 1 July 1916 after very hard fighting at Dantzig Alley and other points, and the cemetery was begun later in the same month. 2,053 Commonwealth burials from the 1914–18 War are commemorated at the cemetery.

On 29 June 1927 HRH the Prince of Wales visited St Bees, and is seen here (wearing a bowler hat) inspecting the 61 men of the St Bees British Legion at the station. The man standing on his left is Lt. Col. George Dixon, president of the local British Legion, whilst just visible behind him is Hugh Lowther, 5th Earl of Lonsdale. Afterwards the prince went on to St Bees School where he inspected the Officers Training Corps, opened the new squash courts at Barony House and laid a wreath at the school's war memorial.

This postcard bears the printed caption 'Flood at St Bees Oct. 20/09' and shows the view from High House Road across the flooded valley. In the week following 20 September 1909, the *Cumberland Pacquet* reported that heavy rains had created considerable losses in the district as a result of flooding. Hardest-hit was the mining industry. In and around Frizington, Cleator and Cleator Moor several mines were flooded and as a result were forced to stop work. It was thought that some would be back in operation soon afterwards, while others would be out of action for some time, with miners unable to work and hardship likely to prevail. The River Ehen and its tributaries overflowed their banks and at Cleator the river flooded mines belonging to Messrs Lindow and the West Cumberland Iron & Steel Company.

This *c*.1920 view shows what is known today as the Adams Recreation Ground. Although it had been used as a sports ground beforehand (a bowling green and tennis courts are visible in the picture), it was officially renamed after the Second World War in honour of Jack Adams, a local trades union official who became Lord Adams of Ennerdale under the Attlee government. The original sports pavilion (visible on the right) stood on the golf course side of the park, and when a replacement was built in the 1960s Jack Adams's widow was invited to open it. This has now been demolished and a new lottery-funded pavilion built. There was also a maypole on the recreation ground and dancing took place around it on May Day. Peck Mill (just visible in the centre of the picture below the church) is referred to in a charter dated 2 February 1211. This forms an agreement between Ranulf of Rottington and Daniel, the Prior of St Bees, which states 'that all his [Ranulf's] men of Rottington shall grind their corn at the Priors mill . . . as the other men of the Prior do'. Although the mill wheel and its race were demolished long ago, parts of the feed watercourse or 'leet' can still be made out leading from near Rottington Hall farm.

14

St Bees Golf Club was formed in February 1906 and was first situated on the links in a location described as 'beautifully and healthily situated on the Nethertown road, within a mile from the village'. A bazaar was held at St Bees School on 15 and 16 August 1907 to clear the debt incurred in building the clubhouse and to provide funds to enlarge the greens and possibly extend the course to eighteen holes. At the time of the bazaar the nine-hole course was 2,810 yards long, with holes varying in length from 125 to 520 yards. As well as stalls selling a variety of goods, the bazaar offered a range of entertainments including pierrots, a play, and perhaps most exotically 'Jarley's World Renowned Waxworks', which were to be exhibited on both days at 6 p.m. These were described as 'a triumph of mechanism' and like the other entertainments visitors had to pay an additional fee to view them. A halt was provided for a short time by the Furness Railway to allow golfers to travel by train to the course. The present golf course on the Lesser Heads came into being in 1928 and is also a nine-hole course.

Until the middle of the nineteenth century Seacote was a farm, but following the arrival of the railway at St Bees in 1849 the Seacote Hotel was built by Lord Lonsdale. Such was St Bees' popularity with tourists in this period that the Lord Mayor of London stayed at the hotel shortly after its opening. Richmond Crescent, to the left of the hotel, was originally going to be grander than it appears today, but its builder went bankrupt before it was completed.

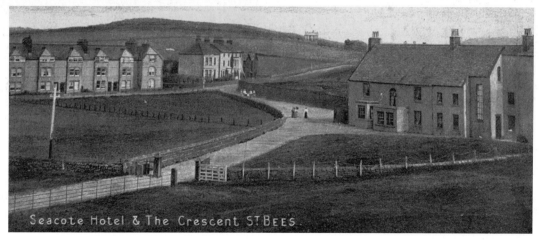

Seacote Hotel & The Crescent St Bees

Originally built as a private house in the 1880s by Alfred Hodgett, Abbots Court was bought by Harry Ashley Brownrigg and his wife Agnes in 1930 and converted into a hotel which gained a reputation for being one of the best in West Cumberland. The brochure from the 1930s recalls 'Its comfort and convenience when indoors, its attractive lounge and music room with all the other amenities of an up-to-date hotel, including bathrooms and electric lighting; also cellar with the choicest of wines. The Hotel gardens and adjacent farms secure daily supplies of fresh vegetables, cream, butter, eggs and meat. The eating is in line with the best Cumberland tradition.' The large heated greenhouses provided flowers for the hotel, seedlings for the gardens as well as tomatoes, cucumbers, lettuces and fine red and white grapes. A walled garden at the rear of the hotel supplied fruit and vegetables and a small field next to the west wall was used to grow potatoes. Hens and pigs were also kept making the hotel virtually self-sufficient. Old St Begans raised funds to purchase Abbots Court which they initially continued to run as a hotel before handing it over to St Bees School which now uses it as a junior boarding house.

Despite only bearing a cartoon and the destination St Bees, this envelope, posted in 1947, safely reached Harry Ashley Brownrigg at Abbots Court Hotel, for whom it was intended. Harry and his wife Agnes were originally partners with Sam Brownrigg who ran a post-horse establishment at Egremont. The firm had always had a strong association with St Bees, and when the partnership was dissolved Harry and Agnes moved to Ashley House in the village. In 1930 they purchased Abbots Court and turned it into a hotel. Irene Patterson can remember the following verse from when she was at school:

Here's Harry with his charry (charabanc)
And Bill with his Ford
And here's Harry going to't quarry
With his charry on a board.

An article from the *Whitehaven News* of 4 July 1963 recalls that 'Brownrigg's were noted for having the best post-horses in West Cumberland, and the best-kept cabs, digbies, wagonettes and hearses. . . . The horses were largely Harry's responsibility, and he invariably bought them in matched pairs – greys for weddings, blacks for funerals and bays and chestnuts for general work.'

Sent in 1903, this postcard shows sheep being sheared in fields at the valley bottom. Farming has long been an important social and economic activity in the district, and Nellie Steele was a member of a family which farmed at Gill, two miles from St Bees. She was one of eleven children. Until the age of eleven she went to the village school, making the two mile journey on foot; after that she went to school in Whitehaven. Ponies and traps were used for longer journeys, although the roads were unmade and often very rutted. Workers employed on the farm began their day at 5 or 6 a.m., and the household made its own candles using moulds and mutton fat. When the family needed new clothes a dressmaker came to the house for a week and made clothes for all of them. They got their water from a well and were largely self-sufficient in food.

Sent in April 1909, this postcard shows Tomlin House and Beach Road looking east, with the Adams Recreation Ground on the right. In the 1950s and 60s it was not uncommon to see three or four double decker buses arriving from Whitehaven full of children, all of whom were keen to take advantage of the weekend sunshine and ready for a dip in the sea. Pupils from Mill Hill School in London were evacuated to St Bees School in 1939 for the duration of the war. In February 1940 55 boys were being accommodated in Grindal House and another 40 at Tomlin House.

This postcard of Finkle Street was sent in 1912. Edward Walker & Sons, whose shop at 7 Finkle Street is in the middle of the picture, was the oldest-established grocers in St Bees, having been set up in 1850 by Charles Walker. The company made a wide variety of own-label products, but was especially noted as manufacturers of scone flour and pickles. An early twentieth century advertisement lists many products including Walkers' Lemonade Powder, Walkers' 'St Bees' Toffee, and Walkers' 'Early Riser' Baking Powder. The advert goes on to state that 'All the fruit used in our jams is grown in St Bees Gardens, and is boiled within one hour of picking'. Walkers delivered groceries by horse and cart as far as Sandwith and Nethertown. The business changed hands in 1925 when Joseph Goss took over, and was later run by Tom Blenkinsop. The premises occupied by Brownrigg's cab office in this picture (No. 6 Finkle Street) were later used a draper's shop run for many years by Miss Annie Walker, who stocked uniforms for St Bees School and also haberdashery. No. 5 Finkle Street (Lancaster House) was a confectioners which was owned by Miss Hannah Bragg, who also worked as a postlady from 1910 to 1930. Two of her sisters, Irene and Hettie Bragg, learned the trade of confectionery and made wedding cakes, also serving teas in the summer.

Edward Walker had two sons, Richmond, who lived at Richmond Terrace (and wore a monocle), and Joe, who lived at Lonsdale Terrace with his wife Esther and their children. The company's pickle factory was in Finkle Street (where Finkle Hall is now), situated next door to their shop. Walkers' well-known pickles, chutney and sauce were made here, the latter two being bottled in square bottles like those used for HP sauce. The labels featured the quadrangle of St Bees School and the Priory Church. The scone flour factory was situated on the corner of Cross Hill and Finkle Street. It was established in 1900 by Joseph Walker and remained in operation until 1925 with the flour being sent by rail to all parts of the country. The printed caption on this postcard reads 'Walkers' 'Early Riser' Baking Powder Department (Tinning & Labelling), St Bees, Cumberland'.

The caption on this 1905 postcard reads 'Walkers' Scone Flour (loading one of Walkers' Special Trains for South of England)'. The siding where the activity is taking place is now the site of the station car park. Edward Walker (who acquired the nickname 'Chutney Joe' when he set up the pickle factory in Finkle Hall) had an intercom between the flour factory office and shop. After it closed in 1925 Brownrigg's bought the factory premises to garage their new motor charabanc. The pickle factory at Finkle Hall made chutney, sauces and jams. The recipe for the pickles was one used by Tom McKay's mother. Ernie Short worked there as a boy after school, peeling onions, coring apples, wrapping St Bees toffee and washing jam jars. He later became the village coal merchant. The crane in the picture was used to load sandstone from the local quarries onto railway wagons.

This postcard of St Bees station shows the after-effects of the 'great snow' of 1895. In its edition of 14 February 1895, the *Cumberland Pacquet* gave copious coverage of the dreadful snow, stating that 'Nothing at all resembling this [weather] is remembered'. Train services were severely disrupted, while several mines were put out of action by the lack of water (due to freezing) for the boilers used by their steam-powered winding engines and other machinery. The *Pacquet* didn't specifically mention events that affected St Bees, although village life would have been disrupted by the closure of roads and loss of rail services experienced elsewhere. An interesting passage in the article describes the following vision of Whitehaven fishing boats: 'Four Whitehaven trawlers, which had been out in the blizzard, were a source of considerable attraction on returning to port on Thursday. What with their rigid canvas and frozen rigging, and the icy encrustations which embellished the exposed portions of their hulls, one might easily have imagined that the vessels had been suddenly transferred from the Arctic regions. The fishermen, it is unnecessary to say, had a very trying time of it.' In the right background of this picture is Seacroft House, the home of artist J. D. Kenworthy. The St Bees sign on the left of the photograph is now displayed on Station House (centre), now home to The French Connection restaurant.

As a lad in the late 1940s and early 50s I spent many hours in the St Bees signal box talking to Bill Procter the signalman (accompanied by his dog Trixie) and watching the steam trains pass through. Bill lived down Seamill Lane with his wife Flo and his front garden was a picture, full of chrysanthemums. As well as collecting train numbers I helped to open and close the level crossing gates by turning the big black wheel that they were connected to. I also enjoyed taking the tablet down to the trains. Some of the coal trains came through at quite a pace and the engine driver would throw his old tablet onto the platform, stick his arm out and Bill would hook the new tablet (which was strapped into a leather bag with a large handle) around his arm. These tablets were used to ensure safe passage of trains along the single line track (there was only double track at stations), and drivers could only proceed if they were in possession of the correct tablet for the direction they were travelling in. You had to be very careful to keep away when the incoming tablet was thrown from the train. The goods trains mostly carried coal from the Whitehaven and Workington mines and the weight of them as they thundered through the bottom of the valley caused buildings to vibrate. When I later worked in the office at the Station Garage I had to stop writing when the coal trains passed through. Racing pigeons were regularly sent to St Bees by train and at the designated time let out of their wicker baskets. They circled and then sped off in the direction of their home. This was a popular release point for pigeon fanciers in the locality.

Rolling stock on the early trains that passed through St Bees was very mixed, as this train seen at the station shows. The crane on the right was mainly used for loading stone from McKay's quarries up Outrigg onto railway wagons; sandstone quarried there was used for facing the Anglican Cathedral in Liverpool. St Bees sandstone dates from the Triassic era about 230 million years ago. It is highly prized as a building material because of its durable nature, ease of carving, attractive colour and texture and resistance to weathering. It has recently come back into favour as a facing stone and is now commercially extracted from three quarries – at Barrowmouth, Pallaflat and Wilton. Next to the crane were cattle pens, while during the Second World War wagons with goods for Nethertown Army Training Camp were also loaded and unloaded here, as was flour produced by Walkers'. There was another small siding to the far left of the level crossing. This was used as a coal yard, originally by Robbie Rose, then later by Brownriggs, Bill Robinson and then Ernie Short. Robinson was a dynamite expert and the agent who supplied the quarries with dynamite for blasting. He also had the riding school at the Retreat Farm. When Ernie Short required coal he would order a goods wagon-full which would be shunted into the siding. Ernie's wife used to be known as Lady Anthracite. Note the gateposts at the end of Coach Road.

This photograph dates from no later than 1898 when Furness Railway locomotive No. 37 was withdrawn. A 2-2-2T Sharp Steward single driver two class B, No. 37 was built in 1866. All Furness Railway engines were painted Indian red, picked out in black with a fine vermilion line on either side of the black. Buffer beams were vermilion lined in black. The numbers and letters were in gold, shaded with light blue. Oil lamps are visible on the top of the carriages, which were painted dark blue with white upper panels. Waist panels were also white, except on the doors where they were blue. Roofs were light grey.

LMWR loco 5776 and LMS 10146 (formerly Furness Railway No. 129) double head a heavy excursion train at St Bees station in the late 1920s. St Bees was a very popular destination for day trips. Most Fridays during the summer saw a trip from some part of Cumberland, with visitors arriving on trains comprising six to eight carriages which were so long that they had to be moved along the platform to allow all the passengers to get off. The Christ Church trip from Whitehaven used three special trains, and having disembarked the passengers then walked to the beach. Christ Church was in Preston Street in Whitehaven and was founded by Canon Parkinson of St Bees in the 1850s. Similar trips were organised for Whitehaven's Catholic population, and also filled three special trains.

This photograph was taken in 1950 and shows Jack Middleton (left) and Bill Procter in the signal box at St Bees. John Sim recalled how bees in their hives used to be periodically sent south by train from St Bees to Drigg and Bootle so that they could collect pollen from other locations. On one occasion the top came off a hive when it was being put in the waiting room and the enraged bees filled the room and ticket office. A local beekeeper had to be summoned to pacify the bees with smoke, and it took two hours before tickets could be issued again. When this

photograph was taken Jack Middleton lived at 32 Main Street. On 10 February 1950, in a house on the same street, a retired schoolteacher and accomplished pianist called Laura Buller was found dead in her home. She had eighteen broken ribs, severe head injuries and bite wounds. The man responsible for her murder was one Patrick Ridge, a former soldier who lived at Nethertown camp and worked at Sellafield. He had met Laura Buller – seemingly by prior arrangement – in the Royal Oak Hotel less than 200 yards from her home on the evening prior to the discovery of her body. Ridge had been discharged from the army in 1945 as being unfit for service, having been diagnosed with catatonic schizophrenia, and as a result of his unsound state of mind escaped the death sentence following his trial, being detained at Broadmoor instead.

Situated 309 feet above sea level on the north end of the headland, St Bees lighthouse marks the southernmost limit of the Solway Firth. The first light of 1718 consisted of an open coal fire in a hanging brazier at the top of a squat stone tower, adjoining which was a cottage where the keeper and his family lived. This light, although of benefit to the numerous vessels which plied their trade in the area, was understandably not very reliable or efficient. It nonetheless remained in operation until January 1822 when it was destroyed by a fire with the tragic loss of the keeper's wife and five children. The original copy of the drawing shown here is now held at Trinity House in London. The wording beneath it reads: 'St Bees lighthouse – damaged by fire January 17th 1822. Drawn by W. Rooke from a sketch by W. Daniell Sept. 1814. Presented to St Bees Lighthouse October 1869 by G. H. Ainger DD principal of the Theological College, St Bees'.

St Bees was the last of the coal-burning beacons in the British Isles, so 1822, the year that saw the birth of the coastguard service, also marked the end of an era in lighthouses. Later that year another lighthouse was built: a square stone tower incorporating a much better light comprised of fifteen oil lamps with silvered metal reflectors, and recorded as being visible for 30 miles. In 1866 the present lighthouse, a round masonry tower 56 feet high (surrounded by a lantern twice the height of the previous one) and dwellings for two families, was completed. The light, a double occulting, was provided by one burning lamp with several cylindrical wicks placed in the centre of a lens utilising glass prisms and bulls-eyes. Mike Murphy has been lighthouse attendant at St Bees since 1989. His father, Osborne Murphy, was lighthouse keeper from 1969 to 1982.

A meeting was held at the Seacote Hotel in June 1970 which set in motion the establishment of the St Bees Inshore Rescue Station. In September that year the inshore rescue craft arrived from the Royal National Lifeboat Institution's depot at Borehamwood, and was in use annually between April and October when it was returned to Borehamwood for an overhaul. The original boat was a fifteen-foot D Class inflatable craft powered by a 40 h.p. outboard motor. Fund-raising for the lifeboat was organised by the Egremont Rotary Club and £1,500 – more than was needed for the boat alone – was raised,

allowing a boathouse to be built on a site prepared by Ennerdale Rural District Council. The boat was dedicated by the vicar of St Bees, the Revd B. H. C. Wilson. Members of the committee, some of whom also formed part of the vessel's crew, were Mr M. Reed (coastguard); Mr R. McLaughlin (auxiliary coastguard); Mr D. Watson (chairman); Mr J. M. Kane (Egremont Rotary Club); Mr C. Robson (St Bees School); Mr E. Hannah (Assistant Deputy Launch Authority); Mr R. G. Brockbank (Round Table), Major D. Style and Mr D. Sim. Mrs J. Morris was treasurer.

The men in this 1978 photograph are, *left to right:* William Forbes; Leon Goldwater; Michael Goldwater; Ian McDowell; Jack Southam; Jim Wrigley; John Brannon; Derek Ashley; Jim Baty.

The structure in the foreground of this picture was the 'cable hut', associated with the telegraph cable that ran from this point on the British mainland to the Isle of Man. A notice nearby stated how far the cable was situated offshore. The telegraph connected into the English network at the railway station. In the distance on the right are tents belonging to the Boys' Brigade, members of whom came to camp every year on Billy Cottam's field for two weeks in the summer. St Bees Head is made of sandstone, red in colour with occasional narrow bands of white. Some 200 million years ago this area was located just a few hundred miles north of the equator, and it was during this period that the St Bees sandstone was deposited. Sandstone has been quarried locally and used for building purposes for many hundreds of years, with the Romans using St Bees sandstone for door lintels and window sills. Three thousand years ago Neolithic man sharpened his stone tools and arrowheads on this abrasive stone.

St Bees Bay and Lesser Heads looking south, *c.*1930. At low tide at the Seamill Lane end of the beach the remains of three fish garths can be seen. These were built by the monks of St Bees Priory to trap fish when the tide went out. Also visible in this area are the coarse glacial boulder beds and gravel that was transported and deposited here at the end of the last ice age. On rare occasions after a particularly heavy storm has disturbed the sand on the beach, relics from the Pleistocene era are sometimes revealed, with ancient tree roots protruding from the ground. After such storms timbers, an anchor and sandstone discs of varying sizes with holes in the middle have on occasion come to light. The latter may have been millstones from the Sea Mill corn mill.

The low rocky outcrop on the right of this picture, an isolated piece of cliff with grass on its landward side, was called the Round Table. Bob Dodding and Howard Smith recalled the little shop (illustrated here) that stood beside the Round Table and which sold hot water, charging sixpence for a pot to make teas. It also sold lemonade, and was owned by Broomfield and then Joe Rothery who boiled the water in large set pots. The shop was made of an old bus body, with wooden extensions, and in its latter days the roof was very bowed. Joe used to walk back on the top of the cliffs with the silver and his wife walked along the sands with the coppers so that if one of them was robbed the other was safe. Bob Dodding also remembered gravel being collected from the shore; this was hauled off the beach by horse-drawn carts (see pages 40–42). 'It was such hard work for those horses. Poor things, they struggled away to get that cart off the gravel. The wheels used to stick about ten inches into it.' By the 1950s the removal of gravel was causing considerable problems of coastal erosion, but as the shoreline was owned privately the parish council was unable to stop it. In 1956, however, Ennerdale Rural District Council bought the Seacote foreshore from Lowther Estates and shingle removal ceased.

This postcard was sent in February 1911. The bathing huts were situated next to the Round Table, and were put up every summer. Mabel Rothery remembers that 'We liked to watch the ladies going down to bathe. They wore baggy blue serge bloomers with a sleeveless top and a big blue 'mop' cap. ... Also at weekends the coven (periwinkle) gatherers came over in droves and sat below our house (Marsh House) on a green bank by the sea. If the tide was in they all stripped off and went for a 'dook'. When the tide went back they all went on the rocks to gather periwinkles which they carried home in sacks on their backs all the way to Cleator Moor where they sold them to their neighbours.'

The bucket and spade beach c.1900, with Tomlin in the background. This postcard was produced by St Bees chemist W. G. Broomfield as part of his 'Sancta Bega' series. Jack Middleton recalled the coastguard's hut on Tomlin: 'there used to be a flagpole up on the top and on August Monday Sports Day there used to be a Guide's race round the flagpole and back. ... They used to have Cumberland style wrestling too. They also had a beagle show. It was quite a good day. Unofficially there was cock-fighting.' Coastguards lived in the hut during the First World War and the stone building with its wooden entrance was used as a store for cattle fodder prior to its demolition in the 1950s. A new lookout was built in 1938 at the edge of the cliff and was manned by people from the village 24 hours a day during the Second World War. The story is told of how a German plane flew over when Dan Walker and Billy Stephenson were on coastguard duty on St Bees Head. Dan opened fire on it with his Bren gun, prompting Billy to say 'Leave it alone, it's not bothering us'! During the war the St Bees Home Guard included a platoon from Mill Hill School. The art master at the school made a very realistic dummy German plane which was carried onto Tomlin for an exercise. Unfortunately villagers hadn't been told about the exercise and a full-scale alert followed.

This postcard shows the rocks around Tomlin and the sea-water swimming pool that was built by unemployed men from the village during the Great Depression of the 1930s. Many St Bees men were employed in the local mines, and as these either closed or reduced their hours of operation the amount of work available dropped dramatically. Building of the Tomlin swimming pool was overseen by a marine engineer called Isaac Spedding, who enlisted other unemployed volunteers to assist him. Work began in 1933 and a massive 600 tons of rock were first blasted and then removed using a three-ton crane lent by Stout's Foundry. The swimming pool was opened on a hot day in July 1934. Access was free for pensioners and the unemployed, while children paid a penny for admission and adults twopence. By the end of the Second World War, when less manpower was available to maintain and clean it, the pool had become silted up.

Mabel and Sarah Rothery recalled goods being smuggled ashore below the cliffs at St Bees: 'There were big holes on Tomlin where the smugglers went down to an opening in the cliff face where the tide came in, and they carried salt and rum from the ships that ran into the opening. The goods were taken up Gutter Foot to Rottington by horse and cart. They also ran the ship into Fleswick Bay and carried the loot up to Rottington, again by horse and cart. Fleswick Bay was noted for its semi-precious stones, and many people took a picnic there and tried their luck. In the First World War there were ships torpedoed and we followed the tides, picking up all sorts of things, soldiers parcels especially, and one Australian ship carried a load of frozen rabbits which laid on the beach for days till they had to be carted away.' Note the beagle hut at the right-hand edge of the picture.

Undoubtedly the biggest vessel to be wrecked at St Bees was the SS *Izaro*, a steel screw steamer from Bilbao en route from Carthagena to Maryport with a cargo of iron ore. She ran aground in thick fog at the foot of Tomlin on 20 May 1907 and was holed forward. Formerly the SS *Edith* and built by the Grangemouth Dockyard Company in 1890, the *Izaro* had a gross weight of 1,773 tons and was 259 feet long. The Whitehaven Rocket Brigade and lifeboat were both called out, although the crew managed to get off the ship safely without their assistance.

CREW OF SHIP IZARO
WRECKED ON TOMLIN ROCK
ST BEES MAY 07

The *Izaro* was trapped on rocks and the crew reboarded her as there was some hope of refloating her. However, after three days of movement she broke her back; her bow and stern had been resting on rocks, but the middle of the vessel was unsupported and the weight of her cargo caused her to break in half. She was sold for salvage, and the removal of over 700 tons of ore started a few days later using a shallow draught steam lighter sent from Liverpool. This took four months to complete, after which *Izaro* was cut up for scrap. Only the keel and the boilers were left and they can still be seen at low spring tides. This postcard shows the crew of the Spanish vessel who camped on the rocks until the ship was declared a loss.

Gutter Foot Bridge *c*.1900. There is still a footbridge over Rottington Beck at this location at the north end of the promenade. The bridge was one of the first village amenities provided by St Bees Parish Council, the first members of which were elected on 18 December 1894 and which sat for its first meeting on 31 December that year. At the time parish councils were being set up all over England and Wales, and as such were the first democratically elected bodies to be appointed at parish level. For the first time married women could both vote and stand for election, making the new councils an important new feature of local government. One of the council's early initiatives was overseeing improvements to footpaths, and in addition to Gutter Foot Bridge a second bridge was built on the path from Blythe Place to Seamill.

The St Bees Beagles used to be kennelled by the beach where the caravan site is now. Jack Middleton recalled that 'J. J. Thompson used to own them. The hunt used to go all over. They went to Wasdale, Ennerdale and all up and down with the beagles. They were followed on foot. The huntsman was Jack Benson. Eventually they got a wagon which they used to take the dogs about in.' Bob Dodding recalled this contraption, which was pulled by four horses: 'When they went hunting any distance they had this sort of wagonette with bars all round the sides, and they put the beagles in . . . and went off four-in-hand, perhaps away up to Eskdale, or Wasdale hunting, and they'd come back about midnight or one o'clock in the morning blowing their hunting horns down the hill and into the village.'

This photograph was taken at the Seamill Lane end of the beach in 1938/39. A young Eleanor Haile (nee Doloughan) is on the cart keeping the horse, Tommy, in order; he tended to be high-spirited. John Doloughan from Cleator Moor had an arrangement with Lowther Estates under which he collected shillies (pebbles) from the foreshore at St Bees (they were also collected from Coulderton beach), taking them to a hopper at the north end of the beach. The shillies were graded and sold to builders for use in foundations, roads and paths, with Doloughan paying the estate an agreed price per ton for what he removed from the beach. A total of six horses were employed. When a cart was full a second horse was harnessed up to it and it was pulled diagonally up the shoreline to ease the gradient.

J15002   THE BEACH AND HEAD, ST. BEES.

The three horses in this picture (from left to right) are Tommy, Nigger and Boxer. Nigger was eighteen hands tall and had to have a shed built especially for him behind Seamill House as he couldn't fit into the normal stables. He was the trace horse, leading the wagons loaded with shillies up the foreshore. On one occasion Nigger was used to pull out a caravan and wagon which got stuck on the gravel. Due to the heavy nature of the work John Doloughan never bought mares. David Percival, a joiner from Hensingham, built a hopper at the north end of the beach with compartments for sand, gravel and shingle. Horse-drawn carts from the beach were led to the top of the hopper and then backed in and unloaded. Lorries drove beneath the hopper and were filled by the chutes with whichever material was required.

Taken in 1948, this photograph shows Bill Monkhouse and horse Tommy, with Old Marsh House in the background. Bill worked for John Doloughan who also worked Clintz quarry (limestone) at Bigrigg and Catgill quarry (sand) at Egremont. His father Henry owned Bankend quarry, Bigrigg, which was later bought by the McKay family. John Doloughan also owned the old Sea Mill at St Bees which he used as a summer residence at weekends. The shovels used to fill the carts were large and it took 68 shovels of sand to make up a ton, while there were 72 shovels of small gravel to a ton and 70 shovels of shillies to the ton. The weights used to be checked at Haig Pit and were always found to be reasonably accurate. The six carthorses were Tommy, Prince, Nigger, Johnny, Boxer and Bobby. Bill Monkhouse used to be able to put a boiling kettle on the palms of his hands without flinching, as the skin had become so hardened by the tough manual work he did.

St Bees School was founded in 1583 as a free grammar school by Edmund Grindal, Archbishop of Canterbury. The son of William and Elizabeth Grindal, he was born at Cross Hill House in 1519 and spent much of his childhood in St Bees. In addition to founding the school, he left £13 6s 8d (a considerable sum) to the poor of St Bees and his Communion cup to the Priory. In spring 1583 Grindal obtained letters patent from Queen Elizabeth I to found a school at St Bees, and on 3 July produced a set of rules regarding the governance of the school, but died three days after these were published and before the school opened. Land was acquired from Sir Thomas Chaloner in March 1586, being defined as follows: 'All that plot of ground known and called by the name of St Anthony's Orchard, containing by estimation an acre and a half, adjoining unto a highway leading between the same parcel of ground and the church yard of the said Parish of St Bees'. This picture shows the St Bees School tuck shop on the right and the Priory with its old 'butterfield' spire.

SWIMMING BATH,
ST BEES GRAMMAR SCHOOL.

In 1687 the headmaster's house was built as an easterly extension of the original school building, and in 1742 the school's coal reserves were leased to Sir James Lowther for £3 10s per year. The agreement to lease the mineral rights for such a low figure aroused suspicion, and between 1811 and 1816 the lease was investigated with the result that in 1827 it was declared void and the school was awarded substantial compensation. Lord Lonsdale re-roofed the main building in 1820, adding an extra storey to it at the same time. Up until 1844, St Bees School consisted of only this one building, situated on the north side of the present Foundation Quadrangle. Pupil numbers fluctuated between twenty and 100, with local boys educated free and boarders paying fees for their lodgings.

RECREATION GROUND,
ST BEES GRAMMAR SCHOOL,

Using money received at the periodic renegotiation of its coal lease, St Bees School expanded steadily from the 1840s onwards, with the first major building project being the construction of the east and south sides of Foundation Quadrangle in 1844. Between 1884 and 1886 the School House was constructed, to be followed in 1898 by the gym and swimming pool. The laboratories, chapel and new classroom accommodation followed between 1907 and 1910. St Bees School has a considerable reputation for its rugby playing. Rugby rules came to St Bees via the mining towns of Workington and Whitehaven in the late 1870s, and in 1882 the Cumberland County Union was formed, consisting of seven clubs: Carlisle, Aspatria, Eden Wanderers, Maryport, Workington, Whitehaven and Cockermouth. Inter-school fixtures were few and far between in the early days, but gradually grew in number.

This postcard is franked 30 November 1906 and was sent to 1 Vale View, St Bees, with the short message 'Arrived safely'. It shows the chapel of St Bees School being built. A commemorative stone was laid in the chapel on Tuesday 23 July 1907 (a fund had been started some years before this) and the building was dedicated at the same time. The block of buildings comprising the science schools and lecture theatre was also opened in 1907, along with the small common room. The library was built as part of the same scheme. Further extensions followed in 1910 providing three additional classrooms, a music room and an art room.

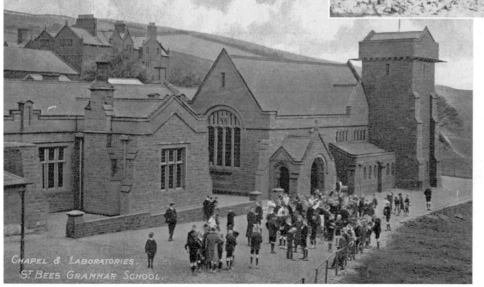

CHAPEL & LABORATORIES,
S? BEES GRAMMAR SCHOOL.

A number of factors led to a period of decline for St Bees School following the First World War. Coal revenues dwindled with the Depression, and with falling birth rates pupil numbers dropped too. At New Year in 1938 it was announced that the school would close in mid-1939 if it wasn't taken over by the County Council, at which point former pupils raised funds and successfully managed to keep it afloat.

Better times followed, pupil numbers began to grow, and following the Second World War St Bees School found itself on a securer financial footing and began to expand again. The Memorial Hall was built in 1954, with New Block following in 1958, the acquisition of Abbots Court in 1973 and girls formally admitted from 1977. This postcard shows the school library, the most ancient and valuable books of which are now held by the University of Newcastle.

This postcard shows damage to Foundation House following the fire at St Bees School on 18 February 1923. The blaze was discovered by pupils whose attention was attracted by smoke coming from the roof of big dorm. Volunteers were rounded up and the local fire brigade had arrived at the blazing building by 2.30 p.m. A telephone message was sent to the Whitehaven and Egremont fire stations at 2.15 and by 2.45 the former brigade had arrived, to be joined by their colleagues from Egremont at 3.10. St Bees brigade, aided by volunteers, had managed to get the blaze largely under control by this time, dousing it with water from Pow Beck, and the fire had been extinguished by 5 p.m. It had originated in a chimney connected with the heating apparatus and quickly spread along the roof of big dorm directly behind the clock tower.